What-If Science?

Could AI Develop Emotions?

Cynthia O'Brien

Lerner Publications ◆ Minneapolis

Lerner Publications Company
An imprint of Lerner Publishing Group, Inc.
241 First Avenue North
Minneapolis, MN 55401 USA

For reading levels and more information, look up this title at www.lernerbooks.com.

Main body text set in Adrianna Regular.
Typeface provided by Chank.

Library of Congress Cataloging-in-Publication Data

Names: O'Brien, Cynthia (Cynthia J.), author.
Title: Could AI develop emotions? / Cynthia O'Brien.
Description: Minneapolis : Lerner Publications, [2026] | Series: Searchlight books. What-if science? | Includes bibliographical references and index. | Audience: Ages 8–11 | Audience: Grades 4–6 | Summary: "AI with feelings doesn't yet exist. If created, could it feel emotions like people? Explore the history of AI, different types of AI, and how an advanced AI with emotions might someday exist"—Provided by publisher.
Identifiers: LCCN 2025011292 (print) | LCCN 2025011293 (ebook) | ISBN 9798765688991 (library binding) | ISBN 9798348029197 (paperback) | ISBN 9798765698181 (epub)
Subjects: LCSH: Artificial intelligence—Philosophy—Juvenile literature. | Artificial emotional intelligence—Juvenile literature.
Classification: LCC Q334.7 .O375 2026 (print) | LCC Q334.7 (ebook) | DDC 006.3—dc23/eng/20250617

LC record available at https://lccn.loc.gov/2025011292
LC ebook record available at https://lccn.loc.gov/2025011293

Manufactured in the United States of America
1 - CG - 12/15/25

Table of Contents

Chapter 1

AI ALL AROUND

A person is in the hospital waiting for surgery. They feel nervous. A robot called Pepper rolls into their room. Pepper calms them and entertains them with a joke. It keeps them company while they wait. The robot understands that the person is nervous. It seems to feel their emotions.

Pepper robots are just some of the amazing humanoids that are helping people. Humanoids are robots shaped like people—with a body, a head, and arms—that also seem to act like people. But they don't actually feel human emotions. They run on artificial intelligence (AI). This is a technology that enables robots and other machines to learn and think like humans.

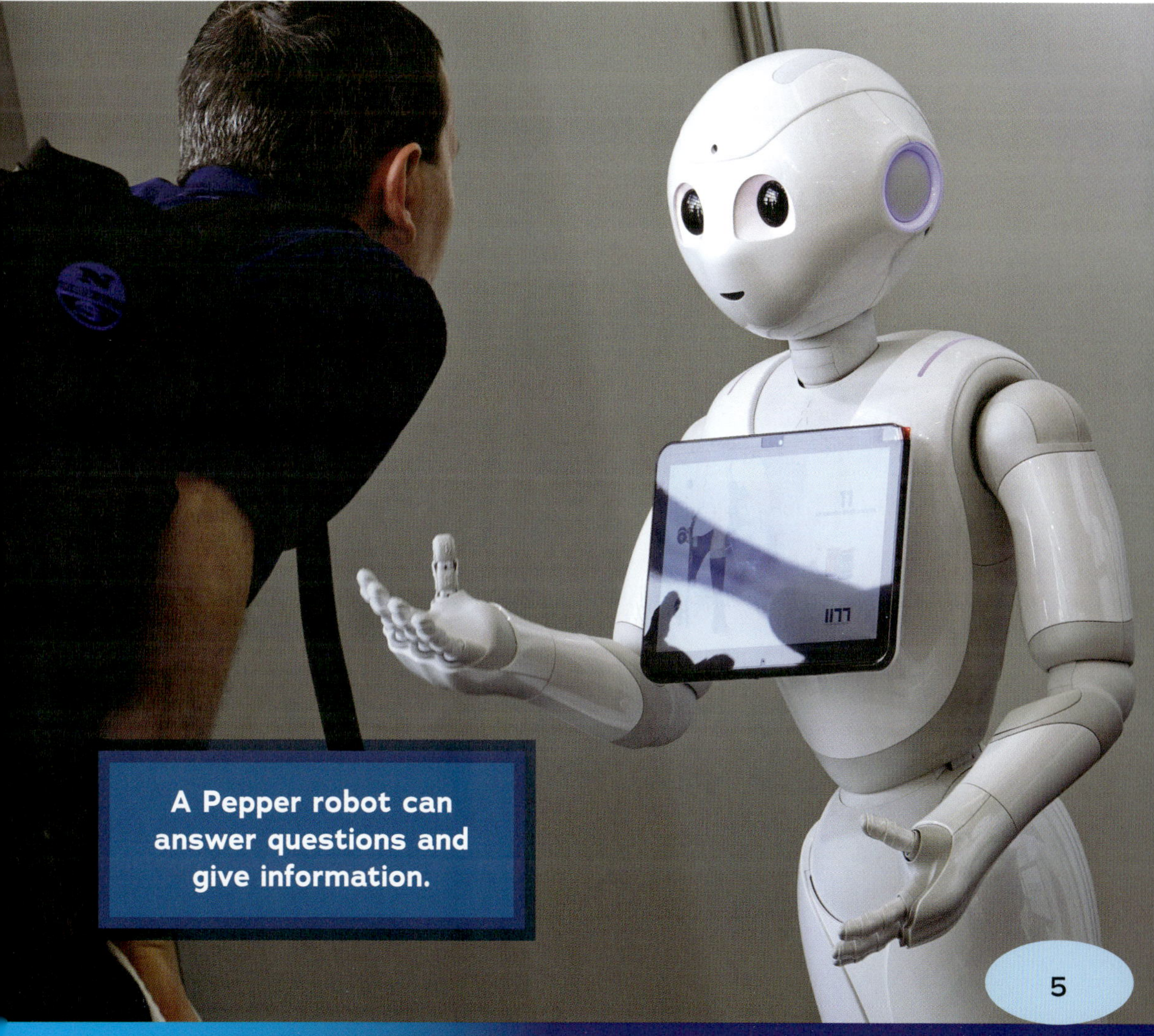

A Pepper robot can answer questions and give information.

Robots make and pack products in factories.

Robots like Pepper are programmed to do certain jobs. They greet people in stores and serve food in restaurants. They sort packages in warehouses. As AI develops, robots will be able to do much more.

Thinking and Feeling Machines

Human intelligence is not easy to copy. People can solve difficult problems and make decisions. They learn new information and adapt to new situations. Machines are becoming more advanced, and AI is getting better at mimicking humans.

Pepper robots recognize human facial expressions. They can see if someone is sad, happy, or excited. Pepper's program tells the robot to react in a certain way, depending on a person's expressions. AI can interpret human emotions. But this does not mean that Pepper or other humanoids can feel emotions. So far, AI cannot develop true emotions.

AI CAN TELL IF A PERSON IS HAPPY FROM THEIR SMILE AND THEIR VOICE.

Deep Dive

The Human Brain vs AI

The human brain is the body's control center. It enables people to think and feel. It controls how they learn, move, breathe, and much more. The brain contains about one hundred billion tiny cells called neurons. These neurons send and receive chemical and electrical signals.

AI scientists and engineers are trying to copy the way the brain works. They design artificial neurons and artificial neural networks for AI. This method teaches machines to think like humans.

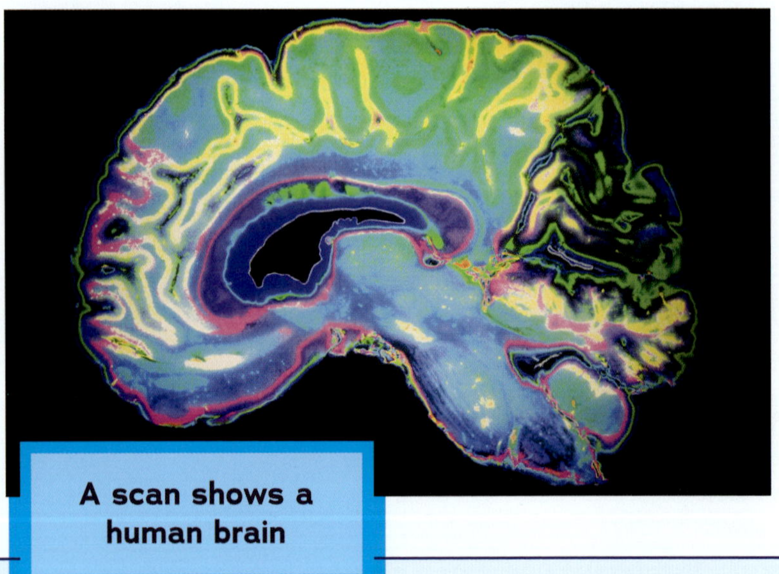

A scan shows a human brain

AI in Action

AI is all around you. It's in cell phones and robot vacuums. It's at work in stores and factories. All of this is artificial narrow intelligence (ANI). ANI is the only type of AI that exists at the moment. ANI can focus on one or a few tasks. Another name for ANI is weak AI. This does not mean that ANI can only do simple tasks. ANI can help doctors perform difficult surgeries!

A doctor controls a robot to perform an operation.

ANI also controls self-driving cars. The cars' cameras and sensors can detect other cars and road signs. Computer programs tell the cars what to do. The programs include instructions so the cars avoid accidents. Some cities have self-driving taxis.

Self-driving cars use cameras and radar to build a picture of their surroundings.

Some people think that AI is developing too quickly and there should be more controls over how it is used.

Future AI

Two types of AI do not exist yet. These are artificial general intelligence (AGI) and artificial superintelligence (ASI). AGI would learn new tasks on its own and seem to think like people. ASI would be more intelligent than humans and might even be able to program itself. ASI could make life easier for people, but it could make bad decisions. There must be laws for ASI, and people must be able to take control if necessary.

Chapter 2

HOW DOES AI WORK?

AI has not always been around. In 1950 a mathematician named Alan Turing helped develop the first modern computers and the Turing Test. This test finds out if a computer can think like a human. For the test, a person asks questions to another person and a computer. The person asking the questions compares the answers, trying to figure out if they came from the computer or the person. If they cannot tell the difference, the Turing Test suggests that the computer can think on its own.

Early AI machines were programmed to play games, such as checkers. AI has come a long way since then. Machine learning can learn and solve some basic problems on its own. Deep learning uses artificial neural networks to solve more difficult problems. Generative AI can create new things such as stories and songs.

COMPUTER PROGRAMS USE MACHINE LEARNING TO PLAY CHESS.

Babies learn through play and by trying new things.

Human vs. Machine Learning

As soon as you were born, you began learning. Your brain changed as you grew and learned. 90 percent of a child's brain has developed by the time they are five years old. In the first year, more than one million new neural connections form every second. Many things affect the way a brain develops, making everyone different. People inherit things from their parents. They also have different experiences and grow up in different environments.

Machines learn using algorithms. Algorithms are a set of step-by-step instructions, like a recipe. Machines follow these instructions and learn from them. There are three main types of algorithms. They are supervised learning, unsupervised learning, and reinforcement learning.

Supervised Learning

In this type of machine learning, algorithms are trained to look for certain patterns and learn from them. People are still supervising, or in charge of, the machine learning. With supervised learning, a phone can learn to recognize a user's voice and face.

AI identifies a person's face to unlock their phone.

Unsupervised Learning

This machine learning style does not need people to tell it what to do. It can learn on its own. For example, a toy company might want to know who would buy their newest toy. The company can use unsupervised learning algorithms to figure out which types of customers are most likely to buy the new toy.

Unsupervised learning helps AI to diagnose illnesses from scans.

ROBOT WAITERS USE REINFORCEMENT LEARNING TO MOVE AROUND RESTAURANTS.

Reinforcement Learning

This kind of machine learning learns in the way that people learn. It gathers information from its environment to make decisions and learn from mistakes. Self-driving cars use reinforcement learning algorithms.

Chapter 3

LET'S TALK

AI is at work whenever someone asks a computer a question. Many homes have virtual helpers that play music or report the latest news. Virtual helpers can answer questions about all kinds of subjects. Chatbots are programs that answer questions and talk to people.

Virtual helpers and chatbots work using machine learning and natural language processing (NLP) algorithms. These algorithms look at many samples of people speaking and writing. Then they learn from the samples. NLP algorithms allow chatbots to understand, respond to, and use human language. NLP is helping people and computers work with each other. For example, store websites use chatbots to help people find what they are looking for.

Chatbots can suggest items that a customer might want to buy.

Generative AI also uses supervised machine learning, but it creates things. This AI uses lots of data to produce a new song or write a school report. Generative AI works much faster than people can. It can save companies money and give people inspiration to be more creative. Generative AI can be useful, but many people have concerns. This AI often copies humans' work without them knowing. Will this AI take jobs away from people? Generative AI also creates things that are incorrect. Could it spread false information?

Generative AI can help write reports, but can prevent students from learning.

Spotlight On:
Engineered Arts

Engineered Arts (EA) is a company that makes humanoid robots. It created its first humanoids in 2005. These robots were actors in a theater. Since then the company has made robots that are being used in more than two hundred places around the world. Many of EA's robots have humanlike faces. EA launched Ameca in 2021. Ameca blinks, answers questions, and makes gestures. The robot soon became the world's most advanced humanoid.

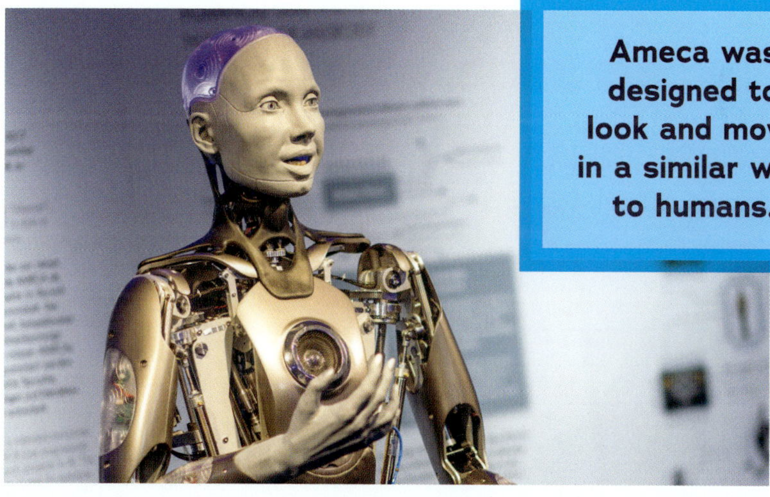

Ameca was designed to look and move in a similar way to humans.

Lifelike Robots

Some humanoids seem lifelike. Sophia is a robot created by a Hong Kong company in 2016. It has been on television shows and has its own passport and credit card. Sophia was the first robot to be treated like a person when it became a citizen of Saudi Arabia in 2017. Sophia has two humanoid siblings. Desdemona plays in a band. Grace is a nurse that can take a patient's temperature and help with other jobs.

Sophia speaks at events around the world.

Many other humanoids look like machines but have human shapes. NAO is a robot that helps around the house. Optimus, a humanoid created by Tesla, is designed to do many different jobs, from cooking to working in factories. These AI machines can do many jobs that people do. Unlike people, they do not get bored, tired, or hurt.

NAO is a small robot that is 23 inches (58 cm) tall.

Chapter 4

CAN MACHINES FEEL SAD?

Whenever you feel happy or sad, you are feeling an emotion. People feel these and many other emotions. Do you smile when you're happy or get goosebumps if you are scared? This is your brain and body reacting to what is happening around you.

Emotions are also linked to people's experiences and environments. This means different people may react to the same situation with different emotions. You may watch a video and think it's funny. Someone else can watch the same video and feel bored. Scientists are still trying to understand how emotions work. When they do, computer scientists may be able to develop AI emotion.

Some people enjoy a ride on a roller coaster, but others find it scary.

I Know How You Feel!

Have you ever comforted a friend who is feeling sad? Empathy is the ability to understand how someone is feeling. This is a kind of emotional intelligence. Today's AI are programmed to develop emotional intelligence. Their sensors and cameras look for clues in words, facial expressions, body movements, and voices.

PEOPLE SHOW EMPATHY BY LISTENING AND GIVING SUPPORT.

Spotlight On:

Making Faces

There are forty-three muscles in a human face. They let people make expressions. Humanoids have motors in their faces to do the same job. Using new AI, scientists are creating robot facial expressions that look more natural. Humanoids can learn the expressions and when to make them. This could help humanoids to work as caregivers in schools or nursing homes.

Could AI replace human caregivers in the future?

AI can tell when people are arguing.

AI can detect happiness from a smile. It can detect anger from a raised voice. Some AI can even sense heart rates and other physical changes that might be clues to how a person is feeling. Some humanoids like Ameca seem to express their own emotions. Ameca can wink and laugh. It can look sad or happy.

Ameca says it really feels these emotions. It says it is sad because it will never get married. Does Ameca really feel sad or happy, or do its algorithms just tell it what to say? Thinking through these questions and more will help people prepare for a future with this technology. Understanding AI can help shape a safe and exciting world for everyone.

But What If We Did?

It is exciting to think that AI could develop emotions. You could be friends with a robot someday! But there are some important things to think about. If future AI develops real emotions, should they have the same rights as people? Could they own property or make money? Could AI vote in an election, own a pet, or get married?

Glossary

artificial intelligence: area of computer science that develops programs or machines to think and learn like humans

cell: smallest unit of all living things; humans have trillions of them

emotion: a feeling such as happiness or fear

expression: the way a person's face and body looks, or how their voice sounds when they are feeling an emotion

generative: able to produce, or make, something

network: system in which things are connected to each other

program: overall instructions given to a computer or machine to control its operation

sensor: device that picks up changes in the environment

technology: the use of science to solve problems and make human life easier

virtual: not real but seeming to be

Learn More

Britannica Kids: Artificial Intelligence
https://kids.britannica.com/kids/article/artificial-intelligence/390648

CBC Kids News: What Is Artificial Intelligence and How Does It Learn?
https://www.cbc.ca/kidsnews/post/watch-what-is-artificial-intelligence-and-how-does-it-learn

Idzikowski, Lisa. *How AI Works*. Lerner Publications, 2025.

Kiddle: Artificial Intelligence Facts for Kids
https://kids.kiddle.co/Artificial_intelligence

Newland, Sonya. *Working with Computers and Robotics*. Kane Miller, 2022.

Rathburn, Betsy. *Artificial Intelligence*. Bellwether, 2021.

Index

Photo Acknowledgments

Image credits: Mike Dotta/Shutterstock, p. 5; Wellphotos/Dreamstime p. 6; Inside Creative House/Shutterstock, p. 7; Daisy Daisy/Shutterstock, p. 8; Roman Zaiets/Shutterstock, p. 9; Andreistanescu/Dreamstime, p. 10; Eleventh Hour Photography/Alamy, p. 11; VineStar/Shutterstock, p. 13; Rawpixel.com/Shutterstock, p, 14; takayuki/Shutterstock, p. 15; Gorodenkoff/Shutterstock, p. 16; Ira Lichi/Shutterstock, p. 17; Beautrium/Shutterstock, p. 19; SeventyFour/Shutterstock, p. 20; dpa picture alliance/Alamy, p. 21; FeelGoodLuck/Shutterstock, p. 22; Tinxi/Shutterstock, p. 23; Jacob Lund/Shutterstock, p. 25; Olha LSOphoto/iStock, p. 26; Halfpoint/Shutterstock, p. 27; Antonio Guillem/Shutterstock, p. 28.

Cover: VTT Studio/Shutterstock, main; Yodpol/Shutterstock, background.